Lovely Legs
JEAN O'BRIEN

To Mary
Hope you enjoy
Jean

salmonpoetry

Published in 2009 by
Salmon Poetry,
Cliffs of Moher, County Clare, Ireland
Website: www.salmonpoetry.com
Email: info@salmonpoetry.com

ISBN 978-0-9561287-2-0

Cover artwork: Girls Night Out from iStockphoto
Typesetting: Patrick Chapman

This book is dedicated to
the women who have fallen:
Marcella, Ann, Susi, Audrey, Breda;
and to those of us still standing:
Peggy, Hilary, Denise, Mary, Carmel.

Acknowledgements

Acknowledgement is given to the editors of *Poetry Ireland Review, The SHOp, Agenda* (UK), *Cyphers, The Stinging Fly, The Oxfam Calendar, Midlands Magazine, Cork Literary Review, Electric Acorn, Revival, The Laois Anthology* (2008), *Southwords, WOW* (Words on the Web), *Stony Thursday*.

'The Stolen Sheela-ná-Gig of Aghagower Speaks' won the 2008 Fish International Poetry Prize.

I would also like to thank the Arts Council of Ireland for their support; Offaly County Council and the Tyrone Guthrie Centre in Annaghmakerrig.

Thanks to Siobhán Campbell and Dixie Friend Gay for their help with some of the poems and ideas for the cover image.

"I am not resigned to the shutting away of loving hearts in the hard ground"

EDNA ST. VINCENT MILLAY

Contents

Masks

A man stands in a field wearing a mantle
of bees. He stands very still, the queen
snared in a cage under his chin.
The black/yellow bodies dance
in the sun, they clamour insistently and stay
very close to him. Their intricate patterns
too complex for anyone to follow.

The sun is a monstrance haloing the skies
and fields are still bordered
with hummingbirds' trumpet, spikes
of orange montbretia and healing yarrow.
These are foreign fields, things gone awry.
The sweep and swoop and drone of the bees
tell of the fields and the erratic flowers,
some from as far as Tierra del Fuego.

Midsummer has been and gone;
The man hangs like a golden apple,
as bees tell each other of the scent
of white yarrow; *millefolium* — a thousand
leaves. They map what they see
with diamond eyes, note
just where their queen is, she is the prize
and the man is taking her on the chin.

Elsewhere a woman wants sunflowers
on her grave. She loves
their pomp and majesty, wants them
to face her and not the sun,
wants their seeds to fall into the earth,
mingle with her marrow and take root.
The man in the mask of bees moves gingerly,
and with a small shake frees himself and leads
the captive bees back to their frame.

The Girl Who Feared Worms

That day it rained, mist lifted from the grass
while drizzle fell back. Worm casts littered
the lawn, she hunkered down with a twig
breaking the skin of earth digging down.
Her beach bucket eventually became
a writhing wriggle of worms, their bruised skin
bulging blue/red bruises, their limb-less
bodies soft and hairless.

Her friend, the doctor, left his door ajar,
light tumbled through the opening,
dust motes speckled the air.
In that moment of lost time longitude
and latitude seemed to intersect
when they crossed paths
and for a moment she stood between
two worlds in no-man's land.

On a square of starched white linen
coiled the lumbricus. The doctor lifted
the knife, the hair on his fingers
standing in the light. He slid the blade
of the scalpel along the full length
of the worm, its threshing stilled
as it metamorphosed into flat ribbons
of red flesh soiling the hanky.

She dreamed night after night
of the scalpel running down pink flesh,
in her dream world she felt its torment
as she became the serpent, dragon, worm.
She sensed the vibrations of the worm's
silent screams, its distress marked
only by its desperate coiling
as it met its own end time after time.

Highwire Act

The trick is to remember that
it is as much in the head as the feet.
Balance is what it's all about.
Fifty feet up it's my world

I climb the hooped rungs
hear the noise of the wind
on my small platform, the big-top canvas
billows in the breeze like a spinnaker.

I think of air as my element
for others it may be water, for me it is air.
I perceive it as solid, dense, something
to hold me up. When I am out there on the wire,

I feel through my feet the taut rope,
that stretches between me and the ground below,
feel its vibrations like a wave through
my salamander feet as they creep blindly along.

I advance and walk the line, motes dance
in the thickened air, my head is in the clouds
and my feet on the tightrope
all is well in my world and I never look down.

Hooks

Don't look at me with a wide mouth
gaping and full of hooks, fish-like
and carping. Oh I have poems
as yet unsung spun from shifts
in air and the geometry of sky.

Your full mouth may jape and jibe
I am used to you and your capers.
The leap and cavort of your tongue
and your sunken cheeks all strung
with hooks and lines will not reel me in.

I'll set my teeth against the wind
my words will sally out sprang as can be,
your speech is famine talk
don't come at me mealy-mouthed
and grave-talk Irish.

The Docile Girls

Lin-We lives in Zijin Cheng with the other docile girls, all young
      and slender,
with sleek dark hair, they look like Seals when they bathe.
The palace is so large it is a city; the Imperial or Forbidden city,
it has many rooms and building and terraces and pavilions.
Except for young Shunzhi our esteemed Emperor no man may live here
      after dark.

In daytime the sun travels from over her building to the Western Gate,
past halls paved with golden bricks and on over Golden Water river
with its white marble balustrades quarried from Lin-We's hometown
of Fang Shan. When the last of the light sinks down behind the
      magnolia trees
all the mandarins and clerks and grooms leave.

At night there are only the docile girls and the eunuchs,
those lost boys, who were docked in the service of the Divine Emperor.
Lin-We thought her lot was better, there were so many girls here
that the young Emperor had only visited her twice.
On those nights the other docile girls prattled excitedly
as they brushed her hair and freshened her breath and teeth with bark,
they lay her on a bed perfumed with rose petals.
The scent was so strong she fell into a torpor.

The Emperor stroked her face and thighs and praised her,
he called her his Lotus Blossom. All the girls knew about that flower
and how it only bloomed its waxy, luminous flower for one short day.
When Shunzhi left her bed the palace sent her mother golden coins
with his face stamped on them as Lin-We had felt his weight imprinted
      on her and felt
again his manhood enter her. She thought about how at night
there is only one penis in the whole palace.

She daydreamed about how someday she would like to walk along
the Imperial Way, but knew no woman may do so except an Empress
on her wedding day and even then she must watch her steps very carefully.

The Chinese Chest

Large and square, the Chinese chest
fetched up here by way of France.
In it I keep my good best china
I thought it suited the far corner.
Its long lacquered doors tell
an old story, of hope and romance
all dressed up with the shimmer
of mother-of-pearl, the ladies dresses
hung in ivory and bone, coloured
in jade and orange blossom.

Its brass clasps with large handle plates
open under an ivory gate and lead
to a garden with a painted pagoda
reached by a small red bridge.
The three swaying ladies clothed
like jewels totter about on tiny feet,
the hopeful swain proffer trays
heaped with trinkets, baubles, bright
things to catch the eye and heart
of any foolish girl.

Cynically I wish them luck hope that for them,
for once, the script would rewrite itself,
but look again at those tiny, tottering feet
and know they will never carry them
beyond that red lacquered bridge
and past the pink cherry blossom
drifting underfoot and out onto
some busy street and bear
them far away. I push the shining pin
into the clasp and close the portals.

Winter Heron

The heron is everywhere now
with the days darkening early
and winter solstice, that old goat,
near, he needs to feed in ever
shortening light. The heft of his wing-
span lifts him lugubriously,
grey feathers are slate against sky.
He flies through a funereal,
persistent drizzle that has been
raining dismally down for weeks.

New lakes magically arrive
cows are marooned on the high ground
as at their feet new streams are born.
The heron has been thrown off route,
these opportunities might prove
fruitful. When he walks in water
he regains his grace, tall and straight
his shoulders hunched, his razor beak
at the ready. If he is patient
at least the fishes might appear.

Winter Dark

Evening leaches light, parcels it up,
holds it tight. Night reverberates.
Winter's hide grows thick
lit by the blaze of dogwood,
the silver bark of birches.
Birds fly on shortened days,
they finish early and start out late
from scarecrow trees whose leaves
have long since fallen.

The wind soughs, branches brush
dusk onto the sky. Flowers
have retreated, shed their seeds
and gone, like a magicians' trick,
back to ground. A late rose clings on,
Erica heather turns from pink to red
in this almost night. Watery sun
cannot outshine the pale lemon slice
of moon that beacons the sky.

The hand on the sundial throws no shadow
in this low light. Colour is eclipsed
by shade. The winter beast bides its time,
it takes the air, spreads its net like tentacles,
a claw of spite. Days crawl forward
heading away from the equinox.
A cradle song hummed in the dark
will move the season on
and spring will break —
a trove of bright.

First Christmas, Cushina

Birds, wind tossed look like silverfish
in mornings pewter light, or the silver
underside of Eucalyptus leaves.

We stood with a forest bearing down
on our shoulders, fir cones crisp
against evergreen trees.

Above a flock of geese flew by
in V formation, they were gaining
height, gathering speed.

Their beating wings
rustling in the breeze,
a whisper just caught

like the sound of a soul
being released,
tossed heavenwards.

We laughed with delight
and shook the clabber of the bog
from our stuck feet.

Later we dressed our tree in tinsel
that quivered metallic
in the rising heated air,

our breath sucked in
we thought we heard faint wingbeats
we stilled our souls.

Spring Equinox

Now the air sweetens with spring
and clouds of starling rise from nearby fields,
their glossy blue-black plumage flaring in morning light.
Today day and night are equal length,
Gossen stones stand testament to time
to the measuring of the days and dates
to rhyme and reason and to all the seasons.

The dawn light on this one morning
struck those grey stones at a precise point,
angels dancing on the head of a pin.
It gave them a moment of startling grace
then the sun set off across the sky
biting back the day.

Almost blocking my sight
the flock of starlings rise like a noisy,
threatening thunder cloud.
They lift and fall dark fireworks
shadowy on my path.
The noise of their cries,
the beat of their wings gathers in
the clear air of spring.

Prevailing Winds

We listen closely to the radio now
for ways of foretelling the weather,
we watch for the hunkering down of cows.

The man who came about the boiler
said the prevailing wind is south westerly.
He seemed to know which way it blows.

It comes snorting and howling
like a stamping beast across the flat
of the bog scattering everything,

even our thoughts before it.
Wind lifts the earth from the lazy beds,
some days it carries the smell of the sea.

Yesterday I found a tiny shell nestled
amongst the gravel, I read the signs
and know how far it travelled.

I could tell what was coming by the way
swallows are tossed to the lee of the house.
The wind unravels words, our tongues are locked.

Our main concern used to be traffic news;
which junction and where was blocked
by the volume of cars?

Here everything is tied down
even on clear days we scan the skies
the siege mentality — our little civil wars.

Born Yesterday

Early morning sun throws long shadows
on the summer meadow, in tall rye grass poppies
and buttercups cluster. Yellow canola's pungent smell
mixes with the cloying scent of wild garlic
growing at the foot of snowy whitethorn.
An eight legged mare forages in a field
her colt ghosting her to ensure she does
not slip away, you would think he had been born
yesterday, he was born yesterday,
perhaps it's a colt pixy, a hobgoblin
come to lure her to the bog. I am walking the dog.
He sniffs and after some digging unearths
the lower half of a black lambs' leg,
ending in a perfect cloven hoof.

Earlier in the year this lane was littered
with double decker frogs, mating as if their lives
depended on it. They marked out a fat green line
as they expanded to catch warmth from the spring sun.
We sidestepped this highway of life
as if on stepping stones, everywhere we looked
were bloated bodies, webbed feet
and not a croak out of anyone.

Then a casualty, I trod unaware on two heaving
bodies and shuddered in horror at the slime and squelch,
the rest of the day was a purgatory of guilt.
By nightfall they had cleared off and the nearby river
was all cloudy with spawn. This leap into the unknown,
this gelatinous mess burrowing into silt,
is like the dog's serendipity.
His lamb's leg is a prized possession,
he will not give it up. How the instinct
for blood makes him hang on.

Uncharted Lanes

We could travel all the redbrick lanes
behind houses in roads with names like;
Palmerston, Windsor or Ormond
they had no ordinance, did not appear on maps
or not the ones we were using, we could spy into the backs
of houses that from the front gave nothing away.
Here were old shed doors painted cherry red or apple green
or galvanised steel garage doors that went 'up and over'.
From where we walked we could see into scullery windows
and gardens that had apple trees, or bushes of gooseberries
or trees with swings hung from them.
Some garden's sported a snagged tennis net.

Sometimes we'd see a pond overgrown with mossy
stones half submerged and we could spy
into a garden shed, its cobwebbed junk taking
on a significance not found in our own sheds.
That cardboard box with faded writing
must contain something more precious than old/
new kitchen tiles that were surplus to requirements.
We liked the uncharted lanes and byways, only children
and dogs in a hurry used them. Once a terrible man,
dressed in a Greatcoat and wheeling a bicycle came along,
he had one hand on the saddle and the other tugged
at his swollen member. This made us remember
to hurry home for tea. We never spoke about it later
and never told our mothers, we would not have had the words.

When Childhood Broke

Father's words woke us,
he stood on the threshold of our bedroom
our lives a fulcrum 'till he spoke
then the dreadful balance tilted
my sister blocked her ears
Her long drawn out
Noooooo
reverberating round the room
broke us.

I lay marooned, motherless,
my bed, an island adrift,
his words a tidemark lapping at me
threatening to breach the bulwark.

With the receding tide I came ashore
different than before
and softly went to mother's room.
In Rigor Mortis she lay curled,
her hands contorted
as if reaching for breath
somewhere way beyond her.

Atropos had been busy here last night,
and with golden shears had severed
the thread of life.
Later women came and laid her body out;
dressed her in a brown habit
and unclenched those hands,
joined them serenely and bound them around
with rosary beads.

I removed her thin gold band it slipped off easy
and loosely circled my slim girl's fingers.
Now with age its golden grip tightens.

Go In Peace

I pass my dead father's parish church,
a quiet morning, a Dublin suburb,
his childhood home nearby, my childhood
home not far. I am leaving Dublin.

I push the high polished door and enter
the hush of the church, firefly light
from candles glints on the golden orb
of the Child of Prague. Our Lady in forget-me-not
blue gazes over. In benches a few grey haired souls
are engulfed in limbo light as they kneel
in the comfortless pews. A rotund priest
cloaked in chasuble and alb intones
the mass, a magic of Latin long lost
comes rushing back.

This near empty church would once
have been awash with people, now its relevance
is almost gone like a lie that continued for too long.
Ite missa est the meagre congregation rises
as one body and there shining in the low light,
I see a young girl. She is backlit by sun
seeping through the red and yellow hues of stained glass.
Her precious head held in rays of bright,
a monstrance haloing her, dark eyes
glimmer hope.

Outside early buds break through ground
split open by frost, the future flowers of daffodils
held prisoner in straight green sheaths,
the promised yellow trumpets form unseen.

Hibernia, Land of Winter

If you are waiting for a sight of the sun
you would want the patience of a heron,
be prepared to stand, balancing one-legged
above the water for as long as it takes.

Look at the bog, the top crust dried to crumbs
in the wind, white bog-cotton bobbing in the breeze.
Deeper down in the murky brown water,
down and down, they buried butter, bones,
gold, silver, stones and books, leather-bound,
wrapped in the gold of hay.

Lie with your face touching damp grass,
turn you back on the sky
and see the worms turn in the clay.
Watch for the thrush with eyes alert
tensed for the slightest movement,
in an instant he will be airborne again,

while you have to stay grounded,
flattened on the grass and still
with the tilt of the earth,
searching always for summer.

Wash

Driving to the coast, my daughter in the back
imitating the Simpsons' chanting,
Are we there yet? Are we there yet?
I forget what month it was,
it must have been spring;
the trees were budding up,
the firm cups of tulips were holding
their own, while the supplicant hands
of magnolia blossoms were starting to falter.

We arrived as the tide was turning,
drawing sand and shale up and back,
The noise resonating with the rush of water
and the clack of sails slapping the masts.
I was thinking of lost summers,
when I paddled in the same cold Atlantic
that my daughter does now;
and I wondered how that long ago
child been altered. Had the draw of the sea
drowned her, as my girl's childhood is being
washed away, drop by tiny drop.

Caliology or The Study of Birds' Nests

We fit close together
and watch as magpies gather
material for their nests.
In early spring we study them intently
as they fly back and forth with great purpose
everything is black and white for them.
Heaving twigs too heavy for their beaks
they fly perilously on.

And studying all this we nestle
ever closer, your hand gentle
as a brush of wing nudges the tangle
of hair, and I am there
with the birds high above the ground.
My rushed breath scattered
and the only sound that matters
is your low hum
insistent like the song of bees.

Painting Nude

"Nobody sees a flower, really, it is so small we haven't
time — and to see takes time like to have a friend takes time."
— Georgia O' Keeffe

They were flowers not people.
No womanly heft of breast,
no rounded belly, skin tone
luminous against the light,
eyes that might eye up the viewer
or coyly look away.

The artist painted only flowers,
a red canna up real close,
labia-like all flowering lips
and pouting red, luscious,
gleaming, the style and stigma
rising from inside.

Strawberry Feast

I love the red lusciousness
of the strawberry feast,
dipping them into sugar
their tart sweetness
a treat for my lips,
their plump roundness
rolls on my tongue.
juice smears my cheek
I bite deep.

Lotus Time

I stayed for a time
in the land of the lotus flower,
walked the silk road willingly
lived inside the thrum of wind
singing through the bamboo.
I forget my home, my family.
One day I awoke
and found I had been beguiled,
lost in the lustrous white
of its petals, the green
of its leaves
its affinity with water.

Shaping Water

Waters translucent
silkiness shapes itself
around the stone
droplets form as
the woman washes
at the basin cupping
her hands in water
that slides over her
and ripples on the orbs
of her breasts
cascades onto the round
of her stomach
flows into the v
between her lovely legs
pools in her toes
sun slants through
the glass gilding her
in splashes of light
she is a body of clear water.

The Irony of Pigs

Zigzags of lightning blaze the sky
and spark off the ground looking
for a conductor to discharge itself on.
The blue bolt zings and strafes the grass
scorching earth as it zips and surges,
a fork-tongued snake ready to strike.
I lie pinioned by rain that pelts off my back
and the smell of blackened grass fizzes
in my nostrils, I freeze and lie flat and
will not be the rod for this frenzied attack.

The distress of the pigs is palpable
they shriek and run about the sty,
their upturned snouts smelling the wind
the crash of thunder makes them wild.
They see the blaze of lightening as it waltzes
and forks on the iron railing of the pig pen.
Their necks are hog-tied, pigs cannot
stretch to look up at the sky.

The Brightening Air

I would promise peace
were it summer,
but winter is harsh
and nothing will grow.
The days are hopeless
and grey, we can only dream
that nature is constant.
Spring is far off, a chimera,
it will come roaring in
like a lion with the tail
of a serpent.
The moon will rise
and throw light
into the hurt cold
of the garden.
Behind the scenes
the moon and sun
line up to pull
at the ever spinning earth,
making the tides ebb and flow
as they stride across the skies
while we below,
stripped down
to the very bones
of winter
shudder and endure.

Magnetic Poetry

Is very attractive,
but has not enough words to go around.
Snow is there, as is morning and night
winter weather and light,
Bloom and grow, sky and flowers
even puddle.

Daily our fridge exhorts us to:
promise good and peace,
beauty and shine, even rattle
is there, but no hum
just murmur
not even humour.

The family shift the sentences about,
this fridge is interactive
coded messages are posted
in limited language;
you love happy child
was intersected with, behind fire,
Positioned above and below
the word love.
Work it out for yourself
I have run out of...

Words Escape Us

There is one person left
in the whole wide world
who speaks Uru,
she could be dead or dying
even as we speak.
She has kept herself to herself
since the second-last person
who spoke Uru died.
The fact is they had fallen out
years before over something
that was said
and now no longer conversed.
Instead they stared wordlessly
at one another whenever they met.
Left to herself she sang,
her clear voice mushrooming,
lilting and ululating
like the golden frill on a chanterelle.
When she is dying her last words;
THE last words of Uru
will hang suspended
cantillating in the air
as if held in a gibbet.
When she is dead no mourners will utter
a last farewell in her mother tongue,
as they return her to the mute trampled earth.

Skylight

The skylight is two foot square
pictured in it are jet trails that never grow
more than two foot long before they vanish
into the woodwork of the frame.

It is like the Brugal painting
The Fall of Icarus
where wings and all he splashes
into the water at the edge.
What happens beyond, out of sight
is anyone's guess.

At night the blue backdrop
is replaced with inky black.
The first and last quarter of the moon
are cradled in this sky crucible
spankled with stars it gleams
like splintered glass.

Seen from this angle;
(grounded, head upturned),
the slant of light seems to gathers up
day and night, night and day.

Poetry Reading in the Bank of Ireland

For P.M.

The diminutive poet's chin barely clears
the lectern as we below look with upturned
faces towards her. She says 'Excuse me,
I'm standing in my shopping bag'. All this
while she tells of meeting a fox in Merrion Square.
Her shopping bag is green,
she is adrift on a blue speckled carpet and her cargo
of words is stitching the sea to the sky
that is even now pooling in a Superquinn bag.

I am temporarily residing in St. Stephen's Green,
where Bono has the right to keep his sheep
should he have any sheep to keep that is.
"Baah Baah" he quotes Beckett.

Nearby the Iveagh gardens, hidden pleasure gardens
delight me, further on La Touch Bridge traverses
the dirty water of the canal, where Paul Smith
came trailing words and Edna St. Vincent Millay's
name is carved in stone while she has returned
to the shelter of misunderstanding earth far from home.

I take my muse for a walk and take my pacemaker too,
or does it take me? We see Brent geese arrive in waves
like a weather front across the whole of the sky,
skywriting that advertises spring.

The poet makes the long climb past the Truth-Body
out of the bag and reads to us anew
about the View from Under the Table,
while the sun edges over the buildings.
There in the brightening hum of her words
and noise of traffic the clang of tram bells
like a modern day Angelus
calls us all home.

Looking for Flowers

I went looking for flowers to Giverney,
we travelled parallel to long fields of yellow rape
(*Brassica napus*), that stretch to a horizon bordered
with meadows and mighty trees
and land that greens out as far as the sky.

Branches of an early summer Musk Rose (*Rosa moschata*),
ramble the hot stone walls and carry
the scent of summer. Pink and white blooms
tangle with the lilac flush of Wisteria's (*Wisteria*)
pendulous racemes. We enter the garden and see
that bridge traversing the water, those as yet unopened
waterlilies (*Nymphaeaceae*) spangle the surface.

Bed after bed of blooms nearby, a palette of tulips
(*Tulipa*) mingle with the lapis blue of Irises
(*Iridaceae*), pushing the boundaries
with narrow paths in between.
Monet's garden pictured and painted
so many times that it looks familiar to our eyes,
a mix of pigment that we recognise.

Later the bees will come buzzing and busy
among the open flowers, their legs will be bushy
with pollen, as they fly back to the hive to perform
their own dream of transubstantiation.
They see the world with compound eyes.

Fighting Talk

The bright lie togs itself out
in the yellow racemes of laburnum —
a lemon surprise to trap birds and flies,
it spreads its poison gift wrapped.

Truth is a labyrinth, obscured
like the alburnum that lies between
the sapwood and the heartwood
we sense it just below the surface.
The hard outer bark, a polished lustre,
something lacquered over.

When we strip it down;
flense it with our vowels
and dipthongs,
flay it with words
and recite it,
write it endlessly out,
gloss it,
parse it,
in the worm
of our tongues
it still spells out war.

The Mayflower Steps, Plymouth 2007

I turn from the wide sea and look back
at the last of land and at mica sparkling
in the sun-warmed granite of the Mayflower steps.

I tread lightly on the Rib, balancing myself,
growing sea legs. Amassed on the horizon
are yachts with their Spinnakers billowing

looking like an armada of coloured balloons
waiting for the wind to fly them skywards.
All that brightness rising.

Unseen from here people are scrabbling
around on sea-washed decks, ducking
the swinging boom, the snapping main sail

tugging at the sheets and jib with hands
reddened with weals and the rasp
of salt-spray.

They shout to other craft
'*Give Water. Give Water*'
like beggars pleading for alms.

Wash from the stern of the Rib is foaming
out, a silver pathway, the ever dissolving
V converging and folding in on itself.

For a moment I am yawed, thrown off course
by the shimmer and shadow of history
back to another early September morning

when the Brethern raised anchor,
after waiting for the turn of the tide
then charted their course

governed by the north star.
The sextant measuring distances
while their eyes were flooded by a vision

they pushed out to sea, with hearts so full
of plans for a New England
they hardly noticed anything at all.

Swimming

My father never learned to swim.
I went with him to the river and watched
envious as boys without fear jumped
from the branch of a tree and struck out
in the water.
When old enough I took the bus
to the public baths and gingerly climbed in.
At high-tide seawater washed over
the concrete sides of the pools,
one deep with a high diving board
and one for young children and beginners.
I blamed him as I waded with the little ones
until I was chest deep, then held my breath
and launched myself, doggy paddling furiously.

I envied other children with a father in tow,
urging them on, propelling them out
and catching them again. It took all summer
before I swam, before I trusted the salt water
and my jerking limbs to buoy me up
as I pushed out into the deep.
I wanted to shout. *"Look at me. Look at me."*
As other kids did and always a father
waiting at the side turned and said
"Very good. Good for you."
I could only urge myself on under my breath.
"Go on, do it again,"
and close my mouth fast
against the water of a running tide.

Timepiece

(i.m. William Willett, who first proposed British Summer Time)

There is a curator of time.
He, and it is a he, exists now as we speak,
not just an idea, a nebulous hazy thing,
but a real person with a job,
the job of minding time.

Of course his place of work is Greenwich
where time is standardised along the meridian,
calculated and regulated. Meantime is the time
after real time. Mean time is calculated from
time past and two hundred atomic clocks.

Not one, not two, not fifty two, but two hundred
clocks ticking away in a place outside Paris,
they divide time down and down until it becomes
indivisible. So mean time is already old time
when we get it to regulate our clocks.

Time out of mind
time after time
time and again
time flies
time enough
time to time
time wasted
time honoured
time bends
time and tide
in no time at all.

Precise time is in retrospect, by which time
it is dissipated. Do you know the stall speed
of a swallow, does the swallow have a stall speed?
Time will tell. Then there is Summer Time
when all our certainties are stood on their head.

Nothing counted anymore when William started
to play with time, he pushed it forward pushed it back
The clock still went tic toc and not tic tac.
The sun still rose in the morning,
set again when it had travelled the full of the sky.
The moon remained the night-time eye
and I only have future time, past time is gone.
All that remains is a limited stretch
of continued existence whether in summer or
winter time, then, like any unwound clock my time stops.

Crossing

You lay rigid
like the stone effigy
of Eleanor of Aquitaine,
hands holding a prayer book
across your breast
just the same.
Behind you at the window
wind threw a squall of rain
like memory,
as if all your possibilities
were alive and well
and not as is,
dead and done.

I sat sentinel all night
to catch what is the thing,
or very moment when the soul
crosses over.
How is the crossing made?
I hoped that if I watched
your hands; bound tight as they were
with beads and busy with the book,
kept an eye on your sleeves
and watched for any trick
of light. I thought then
it would make sense,
From dusk 'till dawn I held the night.

May Altar

The white blossoms were all in bloom
when on the deal cupboard in the back hall,
we made a May Altar, a devotion
to Mary the nuns said in school,
those shrouded figures who damped
down the light of our souls
with their black habits and cowls.

More like something pagan, mother said
observing us filching flowers from gardens
and fields and placing them in jam-jars and bowls.

We borrowed a piece of white lace, or a folded
net curtain for an altar cloth. The chipped
statue of the Madonna in robes of sky blue
was resurrected from a box where she dreamed
time away, only coming out at Christmas
doing duty on display at the nativity scene.

Small Plaster of Paris feet peeping out from her robes
held us in thrall, she was our Queen of the May.
For days on end we visited our shrine:
lighting the white candle that mother gave,
the thrill in the flare of the match, the shine
into darkness, shadows thrown onto walls,
all was magic, prayers didn't come into it.

The sharp smell of sulphur mingled with lily-of-the-valley
until the candle gutted in a puddle of wax
that we dipped our fingers in as if into holy-water,
until it hardened and we peeled off
five white caps. The lilies rotted, the water
in the jar smelled rank. The sun shone, the month
moved on, eventually mother put the statue
of Mary, our May queen back into her box,
and we retrieved the jam-jars to catch tiddlers.

Before

This is a girl of seventeen, a side view,
she is seated on a swing
hung from a chestnut tree
her dress hitched by the wind

This is a photograph of my mother
before I was her daughter
before her father disowned her
before she married my father
before she had six children

This was all before the swinging sixties
that could not free her
before the doctors
before the hospital stays grew longer
and longer,

before they fed the electricity
into her poor head that failed to help her
before the priest offered prayer as a cure
before the shock of her own mother's death
hit home

This is my mother before I saw her
dead in the bed, her cold hands
clutching at air,
before life swung full circle
and could no longer hold her

This is her on that green day
skirt askew, hair streaming out,
holding the ropes of the swing taut
rushing to meet her future
arcing in the air before her.

Felled

This place is in quiet uproar,
A tree has broken rank from the stand
and lies roots exposed on the grass.
It is early, the park is empty,
school children have been and gone
and won't be back until the next bell sounds,
which leave me here with the stricken tree.
Already colonies of beetles are gathering
for a full frontal assault, Lichen is sending out
spoor scouts to test the terrain, everything
is up for grabs. I am rooted. I recognize
this tree, know its branches intimately.

My young self swarmed its trunk,
the branches cradled me between
clear air and green grass that waited
should I miss a step or underestimate
my weight and the sapling strength
of this young tree. I climbed and broke
cover, became part of the canopy
of trees, rows of chimneys rose
from gray slate roofs, the birds
pecking the ground below
looked displaced and I seemed
that bit nearer to the sky.

I made the first cut then, made my mark bite
into living trunk, watched sap weep and felt a pang,
but the urge to leave my name like a three way
secret between me, the sky and tree was deep.
Now I find the initials grown distorted
like loss that warps when left unattended,
the tree tried to heal the breach.
But however faint and however it goes

against the grain, I see those letters
and a younger me clambering higher
than I'll ever be again.
I touch the wound and walk.

The Arc of a Swing in Autumn

When she is seated
the swing's ropes pull taut
then arc from the ground to the sky,
chasing the crest of the moon.
Higher and higher she pushes,
branches hold their silence as wind rushes by.
Shadows scatter and are undone.
She goes to ground: displaced air
hauls its light cargo back.

This is her cradle, her sling. Its highs
and lows hold her in a temporary bow
as she spans the distance between grass
and mid-air. She is shattering the light
of the sun, I hold her image framed
I know it is autumn because the leaves are gone.
All I can see is the outline of the tree,
and my mother on the swing
in the time before me.

Time Traveller

(For my Daughter)

She leans her back into the slats of the chair,
the bars imprisoning her, a pouch holding her in.
The nodes of her backbone strain her skin
and time spools back on a thread.
Her golden head a skull then, bone white,
small enough to fit snug in a hand;
the eye sockets hold the coins
of her green/blue eyes like a purse.

the nub of her heart pulsing like a pinprick,
translucent bud fingers and toes
reaching out past the walls of the womb
grasping her future that has arrived.
She emerged, a human flower,
bright and expected, the kernel of death
sits in under her skin and that skull
will one day be revealed again.

For now she sits with her sea anemone fingers
wrapped around a pencil that she mows
across the white of a page like someone
cutting a lawn in regular sweeps.
She is writing her own story
moving herself into the centre of her life,
not loaned, or copied, or borrowed, just hers.

Frisland and the Dentist

For Jerome Sullivan

I lie in the elongated chair
dark glasses shade me from the glare,
I close my eyes anyway. The dentist
says *open wide*, the needle slides
into my gum, I remove myself from
pain and harsh light and travel
with the old Venetian, Zeno to Frisland.
He holds my hand and shows me wonders.
Green fields stretching out to what seems forever,
lush rivers stocked with fish jumping for flies,
trees aching with fruit; while, dressed in white
like the Archangel, the dentist plunders
my tooth. With a smell of camphor and
the whiff of cloves I leave Zeno
and emerge back to the glow
by the skin of my teeth
and holding my tongue.

The Bailer

Bailers twirling rolls of hay
wrapping them in black plastic,
they spin and dance a strange ballet
the plastic weaving like a modern day
Isadora's scarf,

First the heft on to the tines,
stray stalks billow in the light,
then the whoosh into the air
on rollers. The bales tightly
wrapped in funeral black.
I making tracks
hold my arms aloft elongated
in the shadows of evening
imitating Anthony's angel–
Angel-of-the-North, while the plastic
swirls and swoops like a kite.

Nearby a four x four is herding
cattle, the engine revs and hums
moving them along with an occasional beep
the cows complain with plaintive moos.
I recall seeing a farmer
decked out in wellingtons,
marching stiffly like a child's book
Duke of York, his ash stick
an upright sword, the army of cows
striding full of purpose behind him.
Tomorrow an army of crows
like camp followers will glean the fields
clean and rise up in a dark
dancing puff when we pass.

Dartry

A quiet cul-de-sac
nearby suburban streets
lined with trees and traffic.
The curve of the Dartry road
the tarmac and bus stops and benches,
once it held steel tram tracks leading
back to a depot, long changed in use.
Now an office for Architects
for years though it kept the green corrugated
roof of a permanent gatehouse,
you could almost hear the ring of conductors
clocking in and out. Further down
at the turn of the hill, the old building
of the Dartry Dye Works had a long
stopped clock, that I still looked up at
every time I passed as if it could tell
me something new. Some of the lime trees
that lined the roads were saplings
when I was small, we grew apace
'till they overtook me and flew skywards.
At evening people take their
dogs for walks down by the Dodder river.
The odd toddler, sleepy in a buggy
looks up with interest as a bus
whooshes past all wind and air breaks.
A young woman goes by with earphones
for her ipod, she is wired to her own tunes.

Scandinavian Dream

The dead visit me in dreams
as I lapse between consciousness
and sleep, in that hazy ante-room
where dreams are hung waiting
to be tried on.

Lately my father has come to me,
alive and well it seems after all.
He now lives near some Scandinavian
forest, in a bright log cabin, I see bark
peel from the burnished wood
and trees in the middle distance,
a small clearing like a yard
outside the door with honeysuckle
growing under the eaves.
I could describe this place
enough to go there if need.

The air here is light and suffused
with motes that could be fireflies
waiting for darkness to illuminate them.
My father does not speak to me,
though he is sentient I know
nor seems to notice I am here.
He looks my way but his gaze goes
right through me. He rests
on an upholstered chair,
with orange birds of paradise
embroidered on the upright,
this intricate pattern looks out of place here
where everything is pared down and
uncomplicated. Even if he no longer
knows me, I am glad I have seen him,
he seems content, death suits him in some way.

At daybreak my husband gently touches me
I leave the woods and wake to the summer
cotton counterpane on our bed,
the radio murmuring some unwelcome news.
I fix my sleep filled gaze on a trapped butterfly
tapping its morse unanswered on the window pane.

Night Fright

My bed was positioned just inside
the green door, when mother slowly
opened it I held my breath
until I saw her.
Right next to the bed was a close
patterned wallpaper, which
in parallax view looked a lot
more like a nasty faced goblin
than the trailing ivy paper
I knew it to be.

I sheltered under the heavy quilt
whose paisley pattern also gave fright
if I thought about it for too long.
Just when I was about to get up
and do something about the janus
faced ivy, the hulking door and
to turn the quilt plain-side up
I fell asleep and dreamed
of them all night.

Garden of Reflection

Clustering like noisy doves
sweet Columbines run riot.
A trove of dancing purple Fuchsia
quickstep us into the hush
of the Japanese Garden
of Reflection.
Angular shapes and clean lines
drawing us into the silvered illusion
of a far off garden.

The mirror reflects back clear sky
leading us into another summer.
All is still.
The stark form
of a dead blackbird
lies at the base of the mirror,
he must have flown as if flying
into a vision of himself,
the lush, red smear
spreading everywhere.

The Other Woman

for M.D.

My house is primped and perfect
its best side showing, artfully hiding
its dirty underskirt. Some other woman
owns it now. To her will fall the task
of washing, sweeping, cleaning
again and again. She is taking possession
of all the work it takes to move dust motes
in and out of light.

Early sun catches the front room,
left side corner, does she know that I wonder?
Some morning her spirit will be seduced
by the unexpected play of light on walls.
At night the yellow ball of a full moon
is framed in the Velux roof window,
picture perfect. Someday her fingerprints
will cover every surface,

her footfall every board. The *interconnecting
reception rooms* of estate agent speak
do not convey the life and death dramas
played out in these rooms. She can
possess them now and catch them in the act.
Outside my childhood went missing
somewhere in the garden,
I cried and cried

but it never did come back.
It was laid over by the games and excited
shrieks of my own children. They covered
all my tracks. I want the front door,
with its polished letterbox and handles
to close forever at my back.

Vitreous China

I locked my young self in the bathroom
forgot the lock was rusty and when the snip went
over, that was that, it could not be pulled back.
No-one had missed me, so I rummaged
in the cabinet and found what I was after,
my father's razor. Too small to reach
the mirror, I copied him by touch,
drawing the blade backwards and forwards
across my face, tapping the lethal steel
on the side of the basin that I always
thought said *Virtuous China*, and made
it sing like I had seen him do.
Then a strong stinging sensation
on my skin, it hurt and I wailed,
mother came running and tried to get in,
but the door held. Eventually
father shouldered it, the lock gave
and they came crashing through.
I can still hear her roar as she saw
my face crisscrossed and dripping
with blood. Only then did I remember
that girls don't shave.

Breakage

A mirror was the only thing that broke.
The movers boxed it up in concertina
cardboard and packed it flat.

They stacked it up against a wall
in our new house where it could reflect
a different paint colour in the hall;

windows in another place,
doors that opened in not out,
light displaced, our faces stayed the same.

My husband opened wide the door
the circular mirror started off
rolling fast across the floor,

varnished boards multiplied
repeating themselves over and over
in a silvered sigh it stalled;

paused, stopped and toppled on its front,
we watched with sharp intakes of breath,
its crash. We raised it up

it gave us back our faces cracked,
broken smiles and eyes all splintered.
We hung onto it for luck.

An Abode, Five Letters

In years to come, someone
will take up the floorboards
or unfix panelling from the walls
of this house and find old news
and bills that slipped down
from now, the twenty first century,
just as I found these things
from my father's time.
Mostly flat racing and equestrian magazines,
I found a half-filled crossword,
the inky answers blurred and out
of focus. I felt that if I really
concentrated I could make out
the tantalizing words
as if they might be the solution
to some bigger question.
Perhaps not, maybe
he was just summonsed for tea,
or the carpenter wanted to nail
the last boards down
and was impatient
to be done.

On The Threshold

i.m. Marcella

At first we took it lightly,
hospital pleasantries, soft drinks,
fruit, a small emergency
that added purpose to our day.
As daffodils faded in serried rows,
their fallen trumpets calling
summer, you returned and we
resumed our daily clutter.

Looking paler and a little thin
you turned to the sunlight
browning out the grey etched
in your skin.
Catching sight of your frailty,
as you shrank in the big deckchair,
reminded me of the large house
of your youth and how progress
brought a small terrace;
its redbricked regularity
echoed the narrowing of your life.

We did not know then it would
be distilled even finer. Your body-space
the width of a metal bed
filled with pillows.
The dark form within you
had taken firm root that will
could not shake off, nor yet surrender.
It's not a promise — the three score
and ten, and given choices,
would you want to go
that distance — yet again?

Shadow

This lawn laid out in a large triangle
is cooling your shadow like a sun dial
moving from noon to evening;
you are all sheen and shade
marking time. Your image
is a black silhouette on green grass.
Whatever angle you step out at in the garden
your shadow side-steps you,
like a childs' puppet
its strings stretched and taut.
You sit on the old swing,
its seat mildewed and damp
and pull at the stout ropes
until you move and your shadow
stays swaying with you,
swinging in the insistent air
that holds you in its outline
as it pulls back and forth,
keeping time with you.
You cannot shake it off.
Finally the sun retreats,
a pink glow brightens the horizon
until its light flattens and is gone
the shadow falls
and you go indoors alone.

Cardioversion

'Cardioversion' is a medical term for trying to correct the heart's rhythm with the use of electric shocks.

(for Dr. Peter Quigley)

Sunk in Faraday's Dark Space I try to float
upwards, struggle through layers of ether drift
to blazing light. The air zings with shock,
I am charged, jolted, I have mislaid my beat, its loss
has grounded me, a wild horse, I buck and snort,
leaping as they apply the branding iron that sears
my skin with an unexpected rhythm. They count
the volts, they scorch me and try again with pads
that arc blue electricity from front to back
as it travels the long way through my heart
it stops   and   starts
whipping up a corona of light an aurora borealis
that does not augur well. A runaway horse
I bolt, kick the traces and take flight,
    I cannot
      get in synch.

Back in the ward the Doctor appears like Elector
arcs of light beam out from behind his head.
I shy away. The Doctor, he says that between
the two sharp angles of each shoulder blade
is a perfect half circle, a horseshoe shape
of raised red skin. Now as it heals
it itches in a place
    I cannot reach.

Country Matters

In hot sun this lane dries and hardens
underfoot and dust blowing in from the bog
clogs our eyes. In winter huge tyres
of tractors carrying cattle feed gouge patterns
in mud that frost will crumble and loosen
until the track is impassable.
Once I saw a cow nudging an inert lump
of brown, moaning low she fussed and fretted
circling the still calf until it stirred, moving
its nut brown just-born head and with her
help wobbled to its' new dainty hooves.
The cow licked and kissed it, licking it
into shape, I had just missed the birth.

Farmers traverse the lanes in tractors,
bailers, quads, they meet and greet
one another as if they didn't meet daily.
Nowadays they talk about their herds,
the fields and money while all the while
thinking about the weather. Wondering
how in this landlocked place
all boats can possible rise with the tide.
They ponder on the low rumble they hear,
and question is it the new motorway
passing near or the last gasp of a roar
filtering down the wire from Dublin,
and worry until the hay is won.

Photographing Air

(for Paul Batchelor)

The man who set out to photograph
a kingfisher
might as well try and catch
the colours of a rainbow
with bare hands.
He stays so still, stooks of weeds standing
to attention in the fields,
look like hares
their ears erect, frozen.
But they are not hares,
they are only ghosts.
Things here are not what they seem.

A far off bell reverberates
beating in the rain,
while he sets up the frame,
he snaps—
as in a dream,
the only thing he caught
was a picture of his own hand,
magic like a wand.
His breath uncoiled as he shot
at great shutter speed a shadowy something
that broke from the bank.
Exposed, a blue and orange blur flashed past
astonishing the undeveloped air.

Eyescape

This landscape is flat, broad horizons stretch
out so far that the eye tries to narrow its focus
on something near, it seeks the contours
and undulations, troughs and peaks
no matter how subtle, in these flatlands.

Miles of brown bog and scrub stretch out,
bright water glints and a large flock of starlings
fly to and fro, separate and regroup
like a shoal of fish silverside out
in the ebb and flow of a blue sky backdrop
the furl of wind reeling them in.

At the edge of sight a stand of trees
display their branches where rooks caw and crow
in evening air, the trees are thick with them,
black feathered leaves flail against the green.
The blue yonder immutable like a sea
of tranquillity stretches on.

The Shed

My Russian neighbour Victor
is building a shed, daily I watch him
sawing, hammering, banging.
Generally causing a stir.
At dusk swallows are strafing
the meadow and Victor backlit
by orange streaks of the dying sun,
is firing his nail gun at timber.

His joints are beautifully dovetailed
to resist the wind rolling across
the dark bog that is like the marshes
of Pripet in Bellarus.
Here he is laying claim to a land
that is not home. This shed is his *Isba*.
Light strikes off the distant rows
of turf under black polythene,

clouds shrouding them they look
like far off hills. Rooks setting
off to roost flock in cyrillic lettering
black against the sky;
they write of the Steppes, the distant
Tundra. Victor's axe with its polished blade
slices the high summer air and hits wood
driving a wedge deep to root himself.

The Stolen Sheela-Ná-Gig
of Aghagower Speaks

Set high above the doorway, under the flying buttress,
pockmarked now with age and lately turned to stone,
I sat. Know me I whisper, I am woman, I am crone.
With my etched lashless eyes, hairless head,
grinning mouth and triangular nose how could I tempt anyone?
The wind and rain are always at me, lashing me,
leaving me lonely. Someone saw me and desired me,
swayed by my crude posturing, my endless fertility.
When I open my thighs the world flows in
and the world flows out. I have spent all my life
so far exposed above Aghagower perched in my place
knowing the world through the spread of my lips.
In the unconditional dark someone dethroned me,
un-croned me, made me young and beautiful again.
I shrieked leave me be, I am happy.

Moving My Brother's Books

There were many, many books
who would have thought
such a thing was possible
as too many books.
They had to be culled,
cropped, cleared out.
Big, little, larger, perfect bound,
leather bound, embossed, engraved
colour plates, hickeys, paper bleeds,
it went against the grain
to clear these small cargos
of knowledge, wit, wisdom.
Take your pick each one
an entire world, a destination
waiting in the pages,
the leaves, the margins,
and the ghostings.
In your mind, typeset words
translate into pictures,
on-going stories running verso recto.
We pack and stack them
like brown cardboard bricks
until we have wall after wall
built of books, then all the chattering
of print and pages stops;
the chosen word,
the lush of books
the boughs of trees
the polished stone
the silence sets.

No Cure

On some far beach where earth and shoreline meet
just as the last echo of the vespers bell sounds,
a woman silhouetted in evening light,
naked but for her silver skin
slips into the water with verve.
We watch like souls waiting
to be saved.

Nearby a golden Balalarmy, bird of fable, flies
to where the earth and sky and water meet.
The dipping sun streaks the clouds vermilion
as his broad wings flap and gather in the slipstream
of a star, Venus or evening star.
It shines like a sinecure, useless
and with no hope for souls.

The Sargasso sea deep with floating weed
weighs the woman down. See the knobbled vertebrae
of her back as she thrashes through its clinging mess,
its seaweed dreams. The golden bird flares
above her, the curve of its beak follows
the line of her back till the bird
and the woman are one.

On The Cutting-Room Floor

Celluloid castoffs glint darkly
on the cutting room floor.
We view the rushes,
positive prints.

The Bluebell wood at Emo
flicks into sight, drifts of flowers
glimpsed through trees,
is like seeing sky

upside down, gone to ground.
The projector whirrs on and pans
the vanishing point
behind and before us,

captured in the image of a speeding car
as the road advances and retreats.
Bede's bird flying from darkness
zooms into light and out again,

tracking a life: focus,
close-up, fade.
The flickering scenes we scrutinise
in this darkened room,

coming into view
the narrow water of the river Sheaf
spooling from the Yorkshire hills
down through the bottom of a garden.

The rushes run on,
we cut and snip clearing away
unwanted footage,
splicing together our own version.

Standing on a jetty in Cornwall
as the incoming tide raises
the river water over the wooden slats
we are standing on.

 A woman glides by
incongruous in a canoe
and shouts she's going for chips
as her oars pull and dip

in the roar of water.
Evening light fades
down behind the trees,
and we, ankle deep in the river

retreat to dry land. We print —
running the film onscreen
over and over rearranging the chronology
until we get the story just right.

Our feet crunching celluloid
we step amongst the cast-offs
that are curling like orange peel
smearing light like a vision on the floor.